ROBERT'S RULES
SIMPLIFIED

ARTHUR T. LEWIS
and
HENRY M. ROBERT

DOVER PUBLICATIONS, INC.
Mineola, New York

Bibliographical Note

This Dover edition, first published in 2006, is an abridged republication of the second (1937) printing of *Parliamentary Rules Simplified* by Arthur T. Lewis, which was originally published by Associated Authors, Chicago, in 1935. The book's contents appeared first as a series of articles in *The Christian Science Monitor.*

Library of Congress Cataloging-in-Publication Data

Lewis, Arthur T. (Arthur Thomas), b. 1891.
   Robert's rules simplified / by Arthur T. Lewis.
      p. cm.
   Originally published: Parliamentary rules simplified. Chicago : Associated Authors, 1935.
   Includes index.
    ISBN-13: 978-0-486-45096-4 (pbk.)
    ISBN-10: 0-486-45096-1 (pbk.)
     1. Parliamentary practice. I. Lewis, Arthur T. (Arthur Thomas) b. 1891. Parliamentary rules simplified. II. Robert, M. (Henry Martyn), 1837–1923. III. Title.

JF515.L545 2006
060.4'2—dc22

2006045432

Manufactured in the United States by Courier Corporation
45096104
www.doverpublications.com

FOREWORD

The object of this volume, as its title indicates, is not merely to recite rules but to explain them. Its purpose is to sift from the multiplicity of parliamentary situations the most common ones and analyze the reason for the rules applying to them. It further traces these rules to a few easily remembered fundamentals, thus providing a basis for a sound and practical working knowledge. In this analytical rather than legalistic approach lies its chief claim for distinction—in fact, its reason for being.

It is important that every member of an organization has a clear and correct view of parliamentary law and its purpose. If the nations of the earth are ever to reach the goal of universal fellowship and true democracy it will be as the individual citizens, in their own affairs, make use of discussion, reason, and persuasion rather than force. The meetings of a parliamentary group constitute an ideal school for learning and practising the principles of true democracy. The argument of "minds many" is defeated by a process which enables the group harmoniously to discover its composite will. Certainly the Psalmist, who wrote, "How good and how pleasant it is for brethren to dwell together in unity," would look with approval upon parliamentary law.

Instead of parliamentary rules being altogether restrictive, they are, in reality, liberative. Stripped to their essentials, their root and base is found to be the one great fundamental, the Golden Rule. One gleam of this truth may cut through the complexity that seems to make parliamentary rules obscure and hard to remember.

The text is based strictly upon Robert's Rules of Order,

Revised, one of the best known and most widely followed manuals of procedure in the United States.

Every member of a parliamentary group should understand at least the fundamentals of parliamentary law, and every member can understand them. In this spirit and to that end this book is dedicated. That it may, in some degree, inspire an enlarged concept of parliamentary procedure—of its necessity, dignity, and simplicity—and that from it the reader may gain an enlarged capacity to serve, whether as member or officer of an organization, is the earnest hope of

THE AUTHOR

ACKNOWLEDGMENTS

The contents of this volume originally appeared as a series of articles in The Christian Science Monitor, and the author gratefully acknowledges the permission of that newspaper to reprint them. Gratitude is expressed also to Mary Redfield Plummer, a parliamentarian of many years' experience and wide repute, for her invaluable assistance in reading the manuscript, and for her kind permission to use, from her work, "The 'Double A' Course in Parliamentary Procedure," the comparison of the nest of boxes. Finally, a word of appreciation to Mr. Herbert E. Thorsen, staff artist of the Monitor, whose illustrations serve so well to lighten the treatment as well as to enlighten the reader.

Contents

CHAPTER I

REASONS BEFORE RULES

Parliamentary Law is perhaps too often taken for granted by the members who enjoy its protection and use its privileges. Not understanding its reasons, they may think some of its provisions are difficult to comprehend. They settle down to make the best of it—as they do the weather. They vote when the vote is called for, and at other times are prone to keep silent.

Another type of member may be suspicious of parliamentary law. To such a one, its rules are a "bag of tricks" with which a few members can run things to suit themselves.

Both attitudes are mistaken. In order that parliamentary law may be properly used and not abused, every member should understand its fundamentals, and every member can understand them.

Parliamentary law is more perplexing than difficult. If it seems hard to follow, the student may be trying to remember rules rather than to understand reasons. In the words of Thomas B. Reed, famed former Speaker of the United States House of Representatives: "If the student has once fixed in his mind the idea that parliamentary law is not a series of arbitrary rules—but a plain, consistent system, founded on common sense, and sanctioned by the experience of mankind—he will have gone far toward understanding it."

If you have difficulty in remembering all the various motions—when they can be made, and when they are debatable—do not be discouraged. Begin with a few of the more commonly used motions. Endeavor to grasp the reason for them—why they came to exist, why they are in order at some times and not others, why they usually require a second, why some can be discussed and not others. You can leave less frequently presented problems to be solved with the aid of a manual of parliamentary law. In fact, such a foundational knowledge will make you more expert in using a handbook of rules.

Fundamentals are more readily remembered than the rules which are based on them. The average citizen may know but few of the laws written on the statute books of his community or state but, as a rule, he is familiar with the Ten Commandments, which lie at the base of civilized codes. A knowledge of the Ten Commandments, and obedience to them, will result in a right course of action in any problem of human relationship. Similarly, a knowledge of the fundamentals of parliamentary law will usually enable a member of an organization to proceed correctly.

The many rules of parliamentary law are really applications to different situations of a few fundamentals. All law is founded on justice, and parliamentary law is no exception. Its foundation is justice to all: the member, the minority, the majority, the absentee, the organization. The great underlying rule is the Golden Rule.

As this basic fact is grasped, the entire structure of parliamentary procedure becomes the practice of obedience, self-control, courtesy and patience. Parliamentary law then becomes a fascinating subject for study and practice, full of interest, easily grasped.

The fundamentals of common parliamentary law may be many or few, depending on how they are stated. The following 12 are generally inclusive, yet brief enough to be easily remembered. These fundamentals and the rules based on them govern all deliberative assemblies, except where they may conflict with special rules adopted by an organization as part of its by-laws:

Twelve Fundamentals of Common Parliamentary Law

1. The organization is paramount. To it belongs the power. Its interest and convenience supersede those of an individual member.

2. All members are equal. Each member has equal right to propose business, discuss it, and vote—rights which cannot be suspended or restricted save in the interest of the whole, and then only by a two-thirds vote.

3. One thing at a time. There can be but one main proposition before the assembly at one time. Only one member can have the floor at one time.

4. Full discussion before action. This applies to all main propositions and may be suspended only by a two-thirds vote.

5. Propositions rather than persons. The objective is the opinion and decision of the group upon the proposition, hence debate is impersonal.

6. Propositions may yield to privileges. Matters affecting the convenience or privileges of the assembly or an individual may interrupt consideration of a question.

7. No discussion for interruptions. Matters of sufficient urgency to interrupt discussion may not themselves be discussed.

8. No discussion for suspensions. Motions which have the effect of suspending a rule are not debatable.

9. No second time in the same form. To protect the assembly against waste of time, a question once decided may, as a general rule, not be presented again at the same meeting in the same form under similar circumstances unless a reconsideration is ordered.

10. The majority decides—usually. The majority decides all ordinary questions, but it requires more than a majority to limit a member's parliamentary rights to introduce and discuss questions and vote, or to suspend or modify (without notice) a rule of order previously adopted.

11. Two-thirds vote for extraordinary questions—such as motions to amend by-laws, to change or repeal (without notice) a motion previously adopted, to suspend the rules, or restrict the rights of members to introduce questions, discuss them and vote.

12. Silence gives consent. The right to vote must be exercised. Silence has the same effect as assent to the will of the prevailing side.

As succeeding chapters deal with parliamentary motions and the rules regarding them, reference to the above fundamentals will enable the student to see the reason for them. It will be seen that these fundamentals protect the individual against autocracy or minority rule; that the only restraint of the individual is in the interest of the whole; and that the supreme right of the group to transact its business in due order and with economy of time is fully safe-guarded.

CHAPTER II

HOW TO ORGANIZE

One never knows when one may be called on to take part in a mass meeting or aid in forming a permanent organization. A logical first question, then, is "how to organize." The first steps are much the same whether organizing a mass meeting or a permanent society.

The call for the first meeting. The persons interested in having a mass meeting or in forming a new club, society, church, or other organization, should thoroughly discuss the preliminaries among themselves, and agree upon the place and time of meeting. They then notify others who also may be interested in joining with them and who are qualified. If it is to be a mass meeting, the notice may be published in the local newspaper. On the other hand, if it is preliminary to an organization with a restricted membership, the call would more probably be through personally delivered invitations. Robert says in his "Parliamentary Law": "The call may specify the class of persons invited and none other need be admitted."

The call to order. When those who respond to the call have gathered, one of the group steps forward and says, "The meeting will please come to order." Theoretically, this may be done by anyone present, but, in practice, by one agreed upon beforehand by those who arranged the meeting.

Choosing a chairman. The first duty of the group is to become **organized as a meeting.** The one who calls the meeting to order should proceed in either of two ways:

(1) He may say, "I move Mr. Blank act as chairman of this

meeting." When this motion is seconded, the **one who offered it** puts the motion to a vote. If it is carried, the person selected as chairman steps forward and takes the chair.

(2) The one who calls the meeting to order may ask for nominations from the floor for one to act as chairman.

The latter method is more courteous and more democratic and is preferable if it does not jeopardize the interests of the gathering.

If these methods seem "cut and dried," realize that as yet there is no organization to be "paramount" (Fundamental No. 1), nor are there any "members" to have equal rights (Fundamental No. 2). There is but a group of individuals, and the best and most equitable method of getting under way must be left to the discretion of the individuals most concerned.

Selecting a secretary. There must be a record of proceedings and some one to keep it. The chairman just elected states the next order of business to be the selection of a secretary. With these two officers chosen, the **meeting** is now sufficiently **organized** to go forward.

Determining the object. In a mass meeting, the call for the meeting is read as soon as the chairman and secretary are installed. The call states the subject of discussion and the discussion is **limited** to that. Resolutions may be offered provided they pertain to the subject stated in the call. Unless there is general agreement as to common parliamentary law, it would be well to adopt some standard rules of order.

In a meeting to organize a permanent society, the object, which should be thoroughly discussed beforehand by those who arranged the meeting, should be presented for the consideration of those present, usually by the chairman. After discussion, resolutions may be offered embodying as nearly as possible the majority opinion of those present regarding the intention to organize and the purpose of the organization.

Arranging for the by-laws. The adoption of suitable by-laws is necessary before the permanent organization is accomplished. One of those present should move to appoint a committee to draft a set of by-laws (and a constitution if one is desired, or secure a charter, if the organization is to incorporate). This usually completes the business of the first meeting. Before adjourning, however, a motion should be adopted fixing the time and place at which to meet again. By thus making provision for another meeting, the preliminary session continues its existence and the same chairman and secretary continue to serve.

At the second meeting the chairman calls the meeting to order, directs the minutes to be read, and after these are approved, states the next order of business to be the report of the committee on by-laws.

Adopting the by-laws. The chairman of the committee on by-laws presents the by-laws and moves their adoption. The chairman of the meeting then requests them to be read section by section. After each section, opportunity is given for the meeting to make changes. After all necessary changes are made in the sections, the question is put to vote on adopting the by-laws as a whole. A majority vote is sufficient to adopt them.

Note, as will be emphasized later, that **after by-laws are adopted**, it takes a **two-thirds vote with notice to change** them (Fundamental No. 11). This is reason for being sure that they are as nearly satisfactory as possible before adopting them in the first place. The by-laws take effect as soon as adopted, unless the motion which adopts them states otherwise.

It is possible for a group which intends to pattern closely after another, to save time by adopting at the first meeting the by-laws of a similar organization, simply making the necessary changes in name, etc. It may then proceed immediately with the remainder of the steps necessary. This practice is not recommended except in rare cases. It is better to take a little more time and work out by-laws "tailored to fit."

Signing the by-laws. The persons who are present and who wish to become members of the organization then sign the by-laws. (If a constitution is adopted as well as by-laws, the constitution is signed.) A recess is taken for this purpose.

Election of officers. After signing the by-laws, those present are "members." The first business of the society, now fully organized, is the election of officers, as provided in the by-laws. Unless the by-laws state otherwise, the permanent officers take office as soon as they are elected.

With by-laws and permanent officers, the organization is complete and ready to transact business.

Incorporated organizations. If an organization is to hold property, it should incorporate. This may be done either in the process of forming or after the organization has been completed and by-laws adopted. The steps vary in different states, and a lawyer should be consulted to ascertain the exact procedure.

In an incorporated organization, the members at the time of incorporation sign the charter rather than the constitution or by-laws. From this comes the term "charter members," although by custom the term is used to describe all original members of an organization whether incorporated or not.

When an organization applies for and receives a charter after it has been previously formed as an unincorporated organization, it becomes a **new** organization in the eyes of the law and members must again be voted in, the by-laws adopted and officers elected, although, of course, all these may be the same as before.

CHAPTER III

WHAT AND WHY ARE BY-LAWS?

The first chapter lists certain fundamentals of common parliamentary law. The rules of common parliamentary law, which are the result of universal experience, are also of universal application. By general usage they govern all deliberative assemblies.

Their universality, however, renders them inadequate, for all the needs of an organization. Some of them may not be consistent with the purpose of an organization. To supply this deficiency a permanent organization adopts special rules which are "tailored to measure," adapted to its own particular needs, and

By-Laws Should Be
"Made to Measure"

which apply to it alone. These rules are called by-laws. Compared with common parliamentary law, they constitute special parliamentary law.

It was the custom at one time to separate these special rules into two groups: the constitution and the by-laws. (The prefix "by" is derived from an ancient word meaning "town." A "by-law" was a "town law" as distinguished from a state law, and so the less important special rules came to be called by-laws and the more important the constitution.) Originally, the rules in the constitution were more difficult to change. Nowadays, it is common practice to follow the same procedure in changing all special rules. Hence, there is no longer need for separation. It is simpler to place all special rules in one group called by-laws. Organizations incorporated under the laws of their respective states receive a charter from the state, which serves in place of the constitution.

The adoption of by-laws is the act that actually establishes an organization. The selection and wording of them deserve the most careful consideration. They should include only those provisions which a group deems essential to its continued existence and which are so important that they should not be changed without notice to members, and then only by a two-thirds vote. The by-laws are arranged in articles which are further subdivided into sections.

By-laws may be as simple or as extensive as the size and purpose of an organization require. A typical set would include:

Article I. Name.

Article II. Object.

Article III. Members.
    Sect. 1. Qualifications of members.
    Sect. 2. Election of members.
    Sect. 3. Dues.

Article IV. Officers.
    Sect. 1. List of officers.
    Sect. 2. Duties of officers.
    Sect. 3. Nominations and elections.

Article V. Meetings.
    Sect. 1. Regular meetings.
    Sect. 2. Special meetings.
    Sect. 3. Annual meetings.
    Sect. 4. Number required for quorum.

Article VI. The executive board.
    Sect. 1. Duties.
    Sect. 2. Meetings and quorum of board.

Article VII. Standing committees (how selected, duties, etc.)

Article VIII. Designation of parliamentary manual to govern in all cases not covered by by-laws.

Article IX. Provision for amendment of by-laws.

In organizations having both constitution and by-laws, the former would be restricted to the simplest and most essential of the above points, while the by-laws would amplify them and include any other rules which an organization deems necessary.

There is nothing to prevent a body from adopting any rule as part of its by-laws, even though contrary to accepted usage. It must not, however, be contrary to the laws of the nation or state. A rule thus adopted becomes binding and supersedes any rule of common parliamentary law on the same point which may be included in the parliamentary manual selected by the organization. Hence, great care should be exercised not to include in by-laws any rules on points already covered in common parliamentary law, unless a different procedure seems advisable.

For example, common parliamentary law decrees that a majority decides most questions (see Fundamental No. 10). An organization may feel it wise to have certain officers elected by a two-thirds or even three-fourths vote. A rule to this effect should be placed in the by-laws. In all cases make sure that the wording of the by-laws states clearly what is meant. For example, the rule just mentioned might be included in the by-laws as requiring a "two-thirds vote of those present." This is not the same as a "two-thirds vote." The former must take into consideration all present. The latter does not count those not voting.

Obviously, there might be a great difference in the result, depending upon which rule governs.

By-laws should not be too easy to change, and yet it should be possible to change them if need arises. Some provision for their amendment should always be included in the by-laws. The usual rule permits them to be changed at certain meetings, by two-thirds vote, after notice of the change has been sent to all members. The notice protects all members from any change without their knowledge. The two-thirds vote makes sure that a considerable proportion of those voting approve the change.

Sometimes an organization adopts a motion establishing a policy or governing its future conduct. If such a motion does not conflict with some previously adopted motion or the by-laws, it may be adopted at any meeting by a majority vote. Many organizations gather such rules into a separate group called standing rules. This segregation is simply a matter of convenience. It does not make such motions more important than other regularly adopted motions. But, like all ordinary motions, these standing rules, if changed without notice, require a two-thirds vote (see Fundamental No. 11 and later chapter on Rescind). They may be suspended, however, by a majority vote at any meeting.

In the order of their importance, the charter ranks highest (or the constitution, if there is one), next the by-laws, and then the standing rules. All take precedence over common parliamentary law as represented by the parliamentary manual; that is, they govern in case of any conflict.

CHAPTER IV

THE WHOLE IS GREATER
THAN ITS PARTS

The next time you take a United States coin from your purse or pocket, glance at the inscription on it. In some form you will find the motto, **E pluribus unum**—"one out of many." Just as the 13 colonies, uniting, formed a new federal government, so a voluntary association of individuals in a common purpose creates a distinct entity—the organization. The members may change, but so long as the charter and by-laws are observed, the organization continues.

"In union there is strength." Through coöperation the members gain many advantages of mutual benefit. In return, however, they should be ready, in some instances, to surrender personal desires for the good of the whole. Every member has the right to introduce business, discuss it, and vote. In return, it is his obligation to obey rules, attend meetings, respect the officers as representatives of the organization, and support the organization in its policies and actions.

A member may legitimately argue and vote against a course of action. If it is adopted, he may make every proper effort to have it rescinded. Once the course of action is determined as the expression of the assembly, every member should support that action. He should not speak or act contrary to it outside the meetings of the organization. If there is a better way of doing the thing than a majority of the membership can see, those who have the higher vision must be willing to exercise forbearance and patience to help their fellow members along the more

13

arduous path they have chosen, or until enough more members have lifted their vision to the point where the more desirable action can become the will of the majority.

All members have equal rights (Fundamental No. 2). As a matter of convenience, the organization selects certain individuals to act for it in carrying out its wishes. As a rule these officers are members, although, unless the by-laws specify, membership is not obligatory. The office is a service to the organization. Membership, not office, endows the individual member with his parliamentary rights.

At meetings, two officers are requisite: one to preside and one to record proceedings. The presiding officer is the means through which a meeting expresses its deliberate will. In earliest assemblies the members sat on benches and the presiding officer occupied the only chair. Hence the authority of the office is vested in "the chair" and not in a person. The one who occupies the chair is often called the chairman.

The duties of the presiding officer, while in the chair, are to call the meeting to order, state the business before the assembly, recognize members and assign them the floor, state the question and put it to a vote, announce the result, and decide points of order. His decisions, if contrary to majority opinion, may be reversed.

The assembly considers one thing at a time (Fundamental No. 3); and the chairman always states what that one thing is. If, while a question is being discussed, a member offers another motion, the chairman decides whether it applies to or supersedes the pending question and, if so, states the new matter as the immediately pending question. A good chairman knows at once whether a motion is in order, if it is debatable or amendable, and what vote is necessary on it.

During debate it is proper for the presiding officer to be seated. He has assigned the floor to someone else (Fundamental No. 3). This is not only a parliamentary courtesy due the member who is speaking, but a consideration to the chairman, who should not be obliged to stand during an entire meeting. He rises, of course, when putting a question to vote and whenever else his duties require.

Because the one in "the chair" acts for the entire assembly, he should maintain strict impartiality. He always refers to himself as "the chair." He does not express any opinion on a question being discussed. If it becomes essential for him, as a member, to take a position for or against a motion, he should leave the chair in order to do so, and not return until the question has been settled. While in "the chair" he does not exercise his right as a member to vote except in a vote by ballot or where it will affect the result. In the latter case he casts his vote only after all others have voted, so that his office will not be used to influence the voting.

A good presiding officer will be well informed in parliamentary law, but discreet and not officious in applying it. If members make mistakes through ignorance, it is well to make correction only when justice to the assembly requires it. If discussion or procedure is obviously contrary to the best interests of a meeting, the chairman should be prompt and firm in enforcing strict parliamentary procedure. If the meeting becomes excited, it is essential for the presiding officer to remain calm. One of his duties is to maintain order.

"The Chair" Has the Authority

The other officer necessary at a meeting is the clerk or secretary. He has the privilege of making motions, taking part in the discussion, and voting. The principal duty of this officer is to keep the "minutes" or proceedings of the assembly. These minutes record what is done, not what is said. The essentials of the minutes are: (1) the kind of meeting, (2) the name of the organization, (3) the time and place of meeting, (4) who was in the chair, (5) whether the minutes of the previous meeting were approved, (6) every main motion that is not withdrawn and whether adopted or rejected, (7) by whom it was offered, (8) all other motions not lost or withdrawn. When the vote is by ballot or is counted, the number of votes on each side should be recorded.

The secretary or clerk reads communications to the assembly (unless there is a corresponding secretary, whose duty it is to conduct the correspondence and who also reads communications), also the resolutions offered in writing, and any other document which the meeting calls for. He should immediately note any motion not offered in writing and be prepared to read it at the call of the presiding officer or assembly.

Organizations whose business continues during the period between meetings have need for more officers than the two just described. The list may run to a considerable number, depending upon the kind of organization and the amount of business transacted. The list of such officers and their ordinary duties are to be found in any parliamentary manual. If unusual duties are required of any officer or any special powers are delegated, they should be clearly set forth in the by-laws.

CHAPTER V

WHAT IS A MAIN MOTION—AND WHEN?

The name "deliberative assembly" implies something to deliberate. This something is properly in form of a motion, which is a proposal put forward by at least two of the members.

There are two general classes of motions: main and secondary. A main motion is usually an original proposition—some action or policy presented for the meeting to consider. After a main motion is before a meeting, out of the discussion, or incidental to it, or interrupting it, may arise other motions which are called secondary motions. There can be only one main motion before a meeting at any one time; but there may be in addition to it one or more secondary motions, which for the time supersede it.

As a preliminary to the understanding of parliamentary law, a member will wisely familiarize himself with the requirements and characteristics of a main motion, which are as follows:

First. It must be in order. That is, it must be offered at a time when no other business is before the assembly; it must not conflict with by-laws or parliamentary rules; it must not conflict with a motion previously adopted at the same meeting; it must not duplicate such a motion or one previously made and rejected (see Fundamental No. 9); it must not conflict with or duplicate a motion previously made but not yet finally disposed of.

Second. A main motion must be made by a member who has the floor. To get the floor, a member arises, addresses the chair, and waits for recognition. The presiding officer recognizes him by mentioning his name or merely by a nod. The member may then state his motion. The simplest form is "I move," followed by a statement of the proposition. The member should then be seated. At this point the motion is the sole property of the member who makes it, and he may either withdraw it or change it.

Third. The motion must be seconded, to show that more than one person is interested in the proposition. The member who seconds need not arise or address the chair or wait for recognition. He may call from his place while seated, "I second the motion."

Fourth. The motion must be stated or repeated by the presiding officer. The chairman arises and says, "It is moved and seconded that" (stating the motion as just made). If there is any doubt as to the motion, the chairman will ask the secretary to read it or the maker to repeat it.

After being stated by the presiding officer, a motion belongs to the meeting. The maker or the seconder can no longer withdraw the motion or the second or change it without the consent of the meeting. It is now in order to discuss the motion, but not sooner.

Sometimes this procedure is not strictly followed, and possibly there is considerable discussion before a motion is made. Or a member may speak at some length, concluding his remarks with a motion. This may be admissible at times, by common consent, but it should be realized that a member who discusses a proposition before it is officially before the meeting in the form of a motion, is assuming a privilege which can be granted only by the assembly. A single objection or point of order obliges the chairman to rule such remarks out of order unless the assembly, by a two-thirds vote, grants the speaker permission to continue.

Fifth. As a general rule, when possible, main motions should be in the affirmative. A question in negative form is liable to cause confusion as to the result of a negative vote. If a motion is made that "we do not accept the invitation," it would be better to reword it that "we decline the invitation," making the effect of an "aye" or "no" plain to everyone.

Sixth. A main motion is always debatable (Fundamental No. 4).

Sometimes business is brought before a meeting by a resolution. This is merely a more elaborate form of motion. A resolution should always be in writing. It may be preceded by a preamble explaining the circumstances leading up to the proposition. The preamble begins, "Whereas," and after giving the explanation ends, "Therefore be it Resolved." The proposition then follows. The one who offers the resolution should hand it to the chairman, or with his acquiescence, to the clerk or secretary, who reads it. The sponsor then moves adoption of the resolution.

Communications also may bring a proposition before a meeting; but this likewise requires that a motion be made embodying the action desired in order to place it squarely before the meeting for discussion.

Most main motions bring something entirely new before a meeting. These are sometimes technically called "original" main motions to distinguish them from certain other motions also classified as main motions, which deal with some past or future

Main Motion Should Be Properly Presented

action of the assembly or relate to its business. A motion to accept or adopt a report of a committee on a subject which has been referred to it, or to ratify or rescind some action previously taken, or to amend the by-laws, and certain other motions which may be found in a manual of parliamentary law, are main motions, but not "original" main motions.

CHAPTER VI

THE PARLIAMENTARY "KIT OF TOOLS"

Have you ever watched the final process in an up-to-date factory before a product is shipped to its destination? Each article passes before skilled workers, who give it expert inspection. Some are immediately passed, others rejected as imperfect. Still others may be laid aside for adjustments that may make them acceptable, or sent back to various departments for further attention.

Compare this to the procedure in a deliberative assembly. Imagine the main motion is the "product." Having been introduced, it may be either immediately adopted or rejected. It may be changed and then further considered. It may be referred to a committee for investigation and recommendation. It may be postponed to allow more time for consideration, or it may be temporarily laid aside.

The series of motions provided for these purposes are important parliamentary tools and among the most frequently used. They are called subsidiary motions.

These subsidiary motions are seven in number. Carrying out the comparison with the progress of an article through a factory, they are arranged in the accompanying chart with a vertical space representing the main motion, and the subsidiary motions which arise out of it arranged horizontally beside it and extending from it.

As may be seen, all these motions arise out of the consideration of the main motion and are used to carry out the wishes of the meeting for its disposition. The order in which they are arranged indicates their "rank," the highest being at the top and the lowest at the bottom. When one of these motions has been applied to a main motion and is being considered, a motion higher in rank is still in order. A motion lower in rank than one being considered is out of order.

There are definite reasons in each case for the rank of these motions. One basic reason is (Fundamental No. 1) that the interest or convenience of the entire group takes precedence over the interest or convenience of the individual or any portion of the whole. To illustrate:

After a main motion has been made it may be moved to postpone it indefinitely. This has the lowest rank of all subsidiary motions, since it makes no provision for bringing the main motion up again. It takes the question from before the assembly and is really a negative vote on the main question. It is consequently in order to make any of the other subsidiary motions since they retain for the assembly the opportunity of further consideration.

After an amendment has been offered, it is still in order to make a motion which refers the question to a committee or postpones it to a later time, since both insure more time for the whole assembly and may further provide time in which absentees may be informed.

Subsidiary Motions	
Main Motion	Lay on the Table
	Close Debate (Previous Question) $\frac{2}{3}$
	Limit or Extend Limits of Debate $\frac{2}{3}$
	Postpone to a Definite Time
	Refer to a Committee
	Amend ‡
	Postpone Indefinitely

Motions in white are debatable. Those shaded are undebatable.

$\frac{2}{3}$ Indicates motions requiring two-thirds vote. These motions are not limited to main motions only but may be applied to ANY debatable motion.

‡ The motion to amend may also be applied to certain motions in addition to main motions. It is also undebatable when the motion to be amended is undebatable.

The three highest motions deal with privileges which should not be exercised except to save time for the assembly or to serve its convenience. Their high privilege gives them their rank.

As may been seen from this chart, after a main motion is offered, it is possible to have all the subsidiary motions also pending, providing they are made in the order of their rank. This, however, does not violate the fundamental "one thing at a time," since when any motion higher than the pending motion is offered, it becomes the immediately pending question and is the "one thing" before the assembly. It remains immediately pending until it is voted upon or until another motion higher in rank is made, which in turn becomes the immediately pending question.

In voting upon a proposition which has brought forth several subsidiary motions, the highest ranking motion is voted on first. If lost, the motion which was being considered just prior to it is again pending and must be voted on. And so on. The motions can be made only in the ascending order and must be voted on in the reverse or descending order. To illustrate:

A main motion is offered and seconded, to install a new heating plant. While this is being discussed, the need for some change becomes apparent. Therefore a motion to amend is offered and seconded. Before this is voted on, a member who thinks the proposition needs more careful consideration moves to refer it to the house committee. There are now three pending questions; but note that only one is **immediately** pending—to refer to the committee. (For the sake of simplicity it is assumed that these are the only motions made, but it should be recognized that at this point any or all motions of higher rank—see chart—are in order if made in proper sequence.) Upon being put to vote, this motion to refer to the committee, if carried, disposes of the entire matter. If lost, the amendment again becomes immediately pending and must be voted on. After the vote is taken on whether or not to amend, the main motion, either in changed form or not (depending upon whether the amendment was carried) becomes once more the immediately pending question.

After a subsidiary motion has been voted on and lost, and before the main motion is finally decided, it would be in order to offer a subsidiary motion of lower rank than the one previously offered, because the higher motion is then no longer pending.

CHAPTER VII

TO POSTPONE ACTION— RIGHT AND WRONG WAYS

In the list of subsidiary motions in the preceding chapter there are three that **seem** to be for the purpose of postponing a question. They are the motions (1) to postpone indefinitely, (2) to postpone to a definite time, and (3) to lay on the table. Actually they are quite different from one another in their effect, and accordingly of different ranks.

The lowest ranking motion is to postpone indefinitely. The name is misleading. This motion makes no provision for bringing the question before the assembly again; therefore its effect is not really to postpone but to **reject** the main motion altogether.

Why should this motion be made? Why not vote negatively on the main motion itself? For the reason that, while the motion to postpone indefinitely, if carried, defeats the main motion; if lost, it leaves the main motion before the assembly.

If those who oppose a motion find that they cannot muster enough votes to postpone it indefinitely, they still have the opportunity to amend it more to their liking or refer it to a committee or dispose of it in some other way. The motion to postpone indefinitely in a good way for those opposed to a main motion to test the sentiment of an assembly without risking the possibility of an affirmative vote on the main motion.

The motion to postpone definitely is several steps higher in rank. If carried it stops all discussion of the main motion to which it is applied, but requires it to be brought up at the future time specified—which may be later in the same meeting or at the next session. This is the proper motion used for delaying action in order to gain time for consideration, for gathering information, or for presenting it before a larger gathering of members. It permits discussion—but not of the main motion. The advisability of postponement, however, may be fully discussed, and the motion is amendable as to the time to which the main motion shall be postponed.

Sometimes a member moves merely "to postpone," a question, when his intention is to have it come before the meeting at a later time. Thus stated, it is really the motion to postpone indefinitely. The chairman should try to ascertain the intention of the maker in such a case and recommend either that a time be specified, or that the motion be to postpone indefinitely, thus making it a complete and proper motion.

Highest in rank among the subsidiary motions and also with the apparent effect of postponing the main motion, is the motion to lay on the table. Its high rank is due to its original purpose, which is to allow the meeting to set aside consideration of a question temporarily, without further discussion, by a majority vote, in order to give attention to a matter of urgent importance. For example, members of a club may be meeting on an evening when the national president of the organization is to deliver a radio address. When the time comes for the address to begin, the meeting may be considering some proposition. It is proper then to lay the pending main motion on the table. The assumption is that this is done in order to listen to the address, the intention being to take it from the table as soon as the address is finished.

It is undebatable because the urgency of the purpose makes further discussion inconsistent and yet it requires only a majority vote because it presumably does not stop debate on the motion forever but merely defers it.

Alas! Fair play and the tenets of parliamentary procedure are frequently forgotten in the haste of a majority to "squelch" a motion emphatically. Seizing upon the great power of the motion to lay on the table, and capitalizing on the fact that it requires only a majority vote to adopt it, opponents of a proposition sometimes use this motion to suppress or "kill" a main motion without giving the minority opportunity for discussion. This violates an important fundamental of parliamentary law (Fundamental No. 4). The right of discussion may not be revoked except by a two-thirds vote. While the effect of this motion is to stop debate by majority vote, the legitimate parliamentary intent is merely to postpone debate.

It should be remembered that the original and legitimate function of this motion is to lay the main motion "on the table" which figuratively is right there before the assembly. The main motion may be "taken from the table" later in the same session or, under certain conditions, at the next session. The purpose of the motion to lay on the table is not to "expel" the main motion from before the assembly.

If a majority wishes to reject a proposition finally, it should be willing in the interest of fair play to register its negative vote after full discussion. If the opponents of a measure are so overwhelmingly in the majority that further debate is a waste of time and is not in the interest of the meeting, the proper step is to move the previous question, and by a two-thirds vote compel an immediate decision on the main motion.

Wrongly Taking Advantage of His Power

It perhaps should be pointed out here that if a majority disposes of a question by laying it on the table, at some time later in the meeting the adherents of the measure may find themselves in the majority and can move to take it from the table and then pass it. Turn about is fair play. This is added reason, however, why opponents of a motion should dispose of it in one of the legitimate ways, in which case it cannot be brought up again at that meeting.

CHAPTER VIII

AMEND AND SUBSTITUTE—
A TROUBLESOME PAIR

Chairman: "It is moved and seconded that the club purchase a set of Shakespeare and Dickens. Discussion is in order."

Member: "I move to amend the motion by adding the words, 'in leather binding.'"

The motion to amend is one of the most frequently used in deliberative assemblies. Often the main motion is not presented in the best form to secure a majority vote. If it has been seconded and stated by the chairman, it "belongs" to the meeting and only the meeting can change it (Fundamental No. 1). This is done by:

1. Adding or inserting a word, phrase, or paragraph.

2. Striking out a word, phrase or paragraph.

3. Substituting a word, phrase, or paragraph, or even a complete motion.

The third form is really a combination of the first two. Strictly speaking, it is not correct parliamentary form to "substitute" except in the case of an entire paragraph or motion. When only words or phrases are changed, the proper parliamentary motion is "to strike out and insert," because both that which is struck out and that which is inserted should be subject to alteration by the assembly before the change is finally incorporated. However, in the great majority of cases, there is no disagreement about this; the motion "to substitute" is adequate, and hence is used here for the sake of simplification.

There are a number of steps in connection with amendments which may give rise to confusion unless the reason for the procedure is clear. For example, it is sometimes asked, "Why is an amendment voted on twice?"

An amendment is not really voted on twice. To make this clear, let us refer again to the comparison with the procedure in a modern factory. Suppose the "product"—the main motion—comes before the assembly placed in a box, which is uncovered so that its contents may be inspected—fully discussed. The vote on the main motion—either to adopt or to reject—is like closing the box and marking the contents either approved or discarded. After being "closed," the contents of the box—the wording of the main motion—can no longer be discussed nor can any change be made.

In the accompanying illustration, the largest box contains the main motion. Note that there is **only one.** While this box is still open—before the vote is taken—it is moved to add "in leather binding." This is a primary amendment, or amendment in the first degree. Imagine the words of this amendment in a box smaller than the first box, also uncovered. It must now be decided whether or not to put the smaller box inside the larger box. The vote on the amendment closes the cover of the smaller box. If adopted, it is placed inside the larger box—thus altering in some way the wording of the main motion. If rejected, it is discarded. In either case, the discussion then returns to the larger box—the main motion.

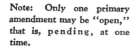

Note: Only one primary amendment may be "open," that is, pending, at one time.

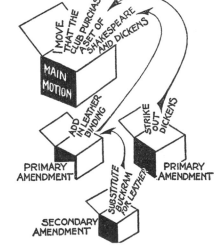

Illustrating **Amend-ments of the Two De-grees**

It becomes apparent then, that the first vote is to adopt (or reject) the amendment, and the second vote is to adopt (or reject) the main motion, whether changed or not.

Now observe in the picture that the smaller box containing the amendment just referred to has below it a still smaller box containing the words, "to substitute buckram for leather." This illustrates how an amendment is itself amended. The smallest box typifies a secondary amendment, or amendment in the second degree. The only time such an amendment is in order is when the primary amendment to which it applies is still open— not yet voted on. The vote on this secondary amendment closes the cover of the smallest box. It is then either placed inside the "in between" box or discarded, depending upon whether carried or rejected. The discussion then reverts to the contents of the "in between" box—the primary amendment.

The picture shows two boxes of the "in between" size, that is, two primary amendments. As many primary amendments as desired can be offered while the main motion is still open, provided they apply to the main motion and are offered and discussed one at a time. Also, while any primary amendment is open, there may be any number of secondary amendments applied to it, provided they are offered and decided one at a time, and provided, also, that they apply only to the primary amendment which is then being discussed. At any given time, however, there can be only **one** main motion open, **one** primary amendment open, and **one** secondary amendment open. Before the main motion is finally closed, however, there may be any number of primary amendments made to it, and to each of the primary amendments there may be any number of secondary amendments.

The final vote on the main motion is taken after all amendments, both primary and secondary, have been decided. After the final vote on the main motion is taken—the cover closed on the largest box—no further changes can be made unless the vote is reconsidered, as explained in a later chapter.

Note: The illustration of the "nest of boxes" is adopted from the "Double A" Course in Parliamentary Procedure, by Mary Redfield Plummer.

CHAPTER IX

DELEGATING DUTIES

In the preceding chapter, the main motion was pictured as contained in a box, the cover of which was to be open as long as the question was undecided. The vote, either for or against the motion, closes the cover. Subsidiary motions may be applied to the main motion as long as it is still pending and as long as no higher motions have been made. That is, the contents of the box may be changed or the whole question—the box, including any changes—can be referred to a committee, postponed to a later time or laid on the table, **if the cover is still open.**

It is often a good plan to refer the consideration of a pending main motion (while the box is still open) to a smaller group of the main body. Such a group is called a "committee," because to it is "committed" some duty or responsibility.

Suppose a main motion is made to install a new heating plant. Obviously this subject deserves careful investigation and study of the advantages and disadvantages of the various types of appliances. To gather the necessary information, to consider the pros and cons, to make a recommendation as to which plant to purchase, are duties which the assembly may well delegate to a smaller group. If no higher subsidiary motion is pending it is in order to move to commit the motion to a committee.

Such a motion may be referred to (1) a special committee, (2) a standing committee, such as the house committee, or (3) the committee of the whole.

A special committee is chosen for a special purpose and automatically ceases to exist when that purpose is accomplished. A standing committee is established to discharge duties which are more or less continuous. The by-laws usually define its duties and provide for its membership and term of office. The committee of the whole is the entire assembly acting as a committee and will be more fully explained in a later chapter.

Frequently the motion to commit is stated in an incomplete form. The motion which refers a question to a special committee should include **four** important things:

(1) The number of members on the committee, (2) how it shall be appointed (unless the by-laws state), (3) what it is to do, and (4) when it is to report. If the motion, as made, does not include all **four** points, the chair may well ask the maker of the motion to include them before stating the question. If the mover does not wish to do so, perhaps having no preference, the four points may be handled as amendments to the motion to commit, before it is put to vote. If neither of these methods is followed, the first business after adopting the motion to commit should be to supply the missing essentials, either by formal vote or by the chair, in an informal way, putting the questions to the meeting.

The motion to commit may actually name the members of the committee, but in this case such names are among the elements that are open to amendment.

While the motion to commit is pending it may be debated, but not the main motion. The debate is limited to the advisability of committing the question, the size of the committee, the instructions, etc. This is no interference with the right of the assembly to debate the main motion (Fundamental No. 4) since, if the motion to commit is lost, the debate on the main motion is resumed as before, and if the motion to commit is carried, the debate on the main motion will be resumed when the committee reports its recommendation. In any case the **assembly** retains its right to make the **final decision** on the matter unless it gives full power to the committee to act for it.

The motion to commit may be amended as to the size of the committee, its instructions, how it shall be chosen and the various other questions pertaining to its organization and work.

Here it should be pointed out that not only main motions

which are pending, but other items of business may be committed to a committee. Two typical cases are:

(1) A committee may be appointed to carry out the wishes of
the assembly as expressed in a motion **already adopted.** For
example, the meeting may vote to tender a dinner to a certain
personage and delegate the arrangements to a committee; in
such a case the box has been closed and it is given to the committee to deliver. Or (2) a subject about which there has been
no motion made at all may be referred to a committee with
instructions to draft a suitable resolution, as, for instance, on the
attitude toward the World Court. This is as if the committee
were asked to bring in the box open, ready for its contents to be
discussed.

Note, however, that in cases such as in the foregoing paragraph, when the subject committed is **not a pending main
motion** (a box with the cover open), the motion to commit is not
a subsidiary motion but is itself a **main** motion and all subsidiary
motions may be applied to it.

CHAPTER X

SPEECH MAY BE SILVER—
BUT AVOID INFLATION

Common parliamentary law provides that there shall be full discussion of a proposition before a meeting decides upon it (see Fundamental No. 4). It is only by discussion, or debate, that members may consider the reasons for and against a proposition and come to a composite opinion about it, as registered by a vote.

It is a general rule that every member has the right to speak **once** to a question. The mover of a main motion or the chairman of the committee whose report is the subject of debate may speak a **second** time. Also any other member may speak **twice**, provided no one wishes to speak who has not already spoken to the question. It is a rule also of parliamentary law that remarks be limited to 10 minutes.

All members have equal rights to debate (Fundamental No. 2), and the purpose of these rules is to protect that right. They assure a **discussion** among members rather than a **speech** by one. The courteous, considerate member will observe these rules himself. If he does not, the chairman need not necessarily refuse him the floor. He should, however, take cognizance of it in granting recognition. If two members rise at the same time, one already having spoken and the other not, the chairman will recognize the latter. If a member who has already spoken twice rises, the chairman, in the absence of any objection, may, at his discretion, allow the privilege of the floor to the speaker, on the assumption that the assembly gives its unanimous consent.

A member will do well to ponder before speaking frequently or at length on a question, refraining in the interest of "the other fellow," unless he is convinced that what he has to say is vital to the whole assembly; and then he should **ask for permission** before speaking. It may not be important that the rules be **always** strictly enforced. It **is** important, however, that a member who speaks more than twice or more than 10 minutes without asking permission shall realize that he is taking for granted permission to do something which is not his parliamentary right and which may infringe upon the rights of others. A single objection or point of order made by a member would oblige the chairman to rule the speaker out of order and require him to be seated, unless a motion is carried by a two-thirds vote, which suspends the rule and gives him permission to continue.

Who speaks first? The maker of the motion (if it is debatable) has the right to the floor first. He may also claim the right to speak last, if he has not already spoken twice.

While full debate is a parliamentary right, it is also a rule that such debate be confined to the question immediately before the assembly. Remarks should always be concerning the proposition, never a person (see Fundamentals Nos. 3 and 5). Personalities should be avoided. Discussion is not between persons. The speaker presents his views to the assembly, addressing them to the chair. If necessary to refer to a member it should not be by name, if avoidable. Officers should be referred to by title.

There may come a time after a motion has been thoroughly discussed when, in justice to all, debate should cease. This is brought about by a motion technically named **the call** or **demand for the previous question.** It is not necessary to understand why this name is used; just remember that it is the same as moving to close debate. In fact, this latter wording is perfectly proper. While generally used in connection with a main motion, it may be used to stop debate on any debatable motion or upon a series of debatable motions.

Since it suspends one of the rights of membership, the call for the previous question requires a two-thirds vote. This vote indicates that many more than the needed majority are ready to vote at once and that further discussion would infringe upon the right of the assembly to transact its business. This should preferably be by a rising vote. If the chair has any doubt about the result, those on both sides should be counted and the count announced and recorded in the minutes. If more than one-third of those voting vote in the negative, the motion is defeated. The discussion of the pending question then continues. If two-thirds vote in the affirmative, the "previous question" is "ordered" and the question on which it is "ordered" is put to vote without further discussion.

The mistake sometimes made is to put the vote on the call for the previous question, and if it is carried, to consider the whole matter settled, including the motion which was being discussed. The affirmative vote on the call for the previous question simply forces a vote on the pending question but does not itself decide that question. Such a mistake is not likely unless there is a large proportion of the meeting in favor of the pending motion and also in favor of voting at once. In any other case, some member opposed to the motion on which the previous question had been

**It Takes Two-Thirds
to Close Debate**

ordered would certainly call the attention of the chairman to the error.

It may be necessary to limit the discussion of a motion to a certain time or to limit the time allowed to each speaker. These purposes are accomplished by the subsidiary motion just below the call for the previous question (see chart in Chapter VI). This is the motion to limit or extend the limits of debate. It likewise requires a two-thirds vote to carry. Neither such a motion or the call for the previous question is debatable, since they have to do only with debate.

"Question! Question!" How often is heard this cry during a discussion. Many persons mistakenly believe that by calling, "Question," they oblige the chairman to put a motion to vote. It has no parliamentary effect and is discourteous if it occurs while a member is speaking or when a member is on his feet seeking recognition.

The chairman should not only ignore it but, if it is persisted in, should call for order. The only time it may be considered proper is when the chairman asks, "Are you ready for the question?" and no one rises to speak. It may then be considered as answering the chairman. Complete silence, however, would have the same effect, as it would indicate that there is no one who wishes to debate further and the chairman would then put the question to vote. It should be remembered that a debatable question cannot be put to vote until all who wish have exhausted their privilege of speaking or until the previous question is ordered by a two-thirds vote.

CHAPTER XI

WHEN THE WHISTLE BLOWS

Preceding chapters have dealt with two classes of motions: (1) the main motion, or an original proposition placed before the assembly for its consideration, and (2) the subsidiary motions, or the Parliamentary Kit of Tools used in disposing of the main motion.

Now we come to a third class of motions which have nothing to do with main motions but which relate to the conduct of the meeting itself or with the rights of some member or members. These are called **privileged motions** because they have the **privilege** of interrupting the discussion of a pending question in order that the assembly may decide a question of greater importance **at that moment** (Fundamental No. 6).

To illustrate, again compare a meeting with the work in a factory. Twelve o'clock comes. The whistle blows and the workmen lay down their tools and stop all work, leaving whatever project is before them right where it is at the moment. So, when a meeting reaches that time when a majority wishes to stop, the motions which enable it to do so have the right of way over any other business and can be made even though a main motion and subsidiary motions may be pending. Because these privileged motions interrupt, they must be decided without discussion (Fundamental No. 7).

There are five privileged motions. On the next page appears a chart which shows their rank. The topmost is the highest in rank, that is, it can be made even though all those lower may have been made and are not yet decided. None of them can be made if any of higher rank is pending. Immediately below the chart showing the privileged motions is the same chart used in

Privileged Motions
Fix the Time to Which to Adjourn*
Adjourn**
Take a Recess*
Questions of Privilege
Call for the Order of the Day

Main Motion	Subsidiary Motions
	Lay on the Table
	Close Debate (Previous Question) $\frac{2}{3}$
	Limit or Extend Limits of Debate $\frac{2}{3}$
	Postpone to a Definite Time
	Refer to a Committee
	Amend ‡
	Postpone Indefinitely

Motions in white are debatable. Motions shaded are undebatable.

* These motions are not privileged if made when no business is pending.

**This motion is not privileged when qualified or when its adoption would dissolve the assembly.

⅔ These motions require a two-thirds vote. They may be applied to any debatable motions.

‡ The motion to amend may be applied to certain motions in addition to main motions and is undebatable when applied to an undebatable motion.

Chapter VI to show the subsidiary motions and their relation to one another as well as to a main motion.

Any of the motions in the combined chart is in order if offered while no motion of higher rank is pending. To illustrate:

A main motion has been made and an amendment is offered. While this is being debated, it is in order to move any of the higher subsidiary or privileged motions, in ascending order, but the lower motion, to postpone indefinitely, would be out of order. If the motion to lay on the table is made, no other subsidiary motions could be made until after it is decided, but any of the privileged motions could be made. The motions are made in the ascending order, and are voted on in the descending order.

In an assembly having frequent regular meetings, or whose rules provide for easily arranged special meetings, there is seldom need for the highest ranking motion, to fix the time to which to adjourn. It is helpful to understand its purpose and power, however, as the occasion may arise for adjourning a meeting to a special time. This motion is in order even though the motion to adjourn is made, seconded, and carried, provided the chair has not actually declared the meeting adjourned. Its high privilege is because the right of the majority to provide for an essential continuation of a meeting is higher than its right to adjourn a meeting.

If the assembly sees the need for an adjourned meeting, it is better to offer the motion to fix the time to which to adjourn when there is no business pending. The motion then has no privilege, there being nothing for it to interrupt, and is an ordinary main motion, which may be debated, and have all subsidiary motions applied to it.

Because the motion to fix the time to which to adjourn is seldom necessary, many persons erroneously believe that the motion to adjourn is the highest of all motions. As the chart shows, it is next highest.

Whether it interrupts discussion or not, the motion to adjourn is always privileged except (1) when it is qualified, as for example "to adjourn at 2 o'clock" (obviously such a motion does not oblige a meeting to stop all discussion immediately, hence it is an ordinary debatable and amendable main motion); (2) if it closes the session of an assembly which has no provision for future sessions. In every permanent society, however, the by-laws provide for future meetings. So in the great majority of cases, the motion to adjourn is privileged.

The privilege of this motion gives it the right to **interrupt business** but not to interrupt a member who is speaking. The motion to adjourn is proper only when made by a member who has risen and secured recognition. It must be seconded. Sometimes this motion is called out by one who remains seated. If then entertained by the chair it can be only on the assumption that there is a general consent to consider it. Members should take care not to fall into the error of thinking that such procedure is always permissible. If the motion is thus called out by one who is seated while another member is on his feet speaking or seeking recognition for some other purpose, it is not only discourteous but has no parliamentary effect. If persisted in, the chair should call for order.

If a meeting adjourns while business is pending, the business falls to the ground in an organization which does not have regular meetings as often as quarterly. It can be renewed, however, at the next session. In an organization having regular meetings as often as quarterly, the business pending is brought up at the next session as unfinished business.

The motion to take a recess is privileged if made while business is pending because if carried it stops business immediately. However, to move at ten o'clock to recess at noon, is not a privileged motion because it does not interfere with business **now**. Also if all pending business has been disposed of, the motion to recess immediately is not privileged.

Another privileged motion is a question of privilege. Be careful not to confuse the two terms. The former describes a general class of motions which have the privilege of interrupting. The latter describes a motion **of that class**, which relates to certain privileges or rights, either of the assembly or of some member.

A member who calls out, "Mr. Chairman, we cannot hear the speaker," is stating a question of privilege. It is the privilege of the assembly to be comfortable, to hear the speakers, to inquire into the conduct of the meeting or its officers. These are questions of general privilege. Questions of personal privilege (which are rare) may relate, for example, to the individual member's right to be heard in defense of himself if his right to membership has been challenged, or if he is credited in the minutes with having made a motion to which he is opposed.

The correct procedure is for the member to rise and say, "I rise to a question of general (or personal) privilege." The chair directs him to state his question and then decides whether or not it shall be allowed. Any two members may appeal from the decision of the chair, in which case the appeal must be put to vote. The appeal, however, is not a privileged motion, but is like a main motion in that it can be debated, amended, etc.

CHAPTER XII

KEEPING ON THE RIGHT ROAD

The lowest in rank of the privileged motions is the call for the orders of the day (see chart in preceding chapter).

A meeting of an assembly might be likened to a party of people who have gathered to take a trip in a bus. The journey takes them over an established, well-paved route with regular stops. If through mistake or in an attempted short cut, the driver should take an unauthorized detour, it is the privilege of any passenger to demand that the regular route be followed.

The road map, as it were, of a deliberative assembly is its Order of Business. This is a plan or program prescribing the order in which business shall be considered. A society may adopt as part of its by-laws or rules of order a special order of business for its meetings. If it does not, the order of business which is set down in the parliamentary authority adopted in its by-laws shall be followed.

The following is the usual order of business in parliamentary gatherings, as set forth in Robert's Rules of Order:

1. **Reading of the minutes** of the previous meeting and their approval. This is naturally first. It shows where the previous meeting left off and what was done.

2. **Reports of Officers, Boards, and Standing Committees** (in the order named). The report of the Secretary (Corresponding Secretary if there is one) includes reading of the correspondence. It is proper for the meeting to take any action that is necessary at the time a report is made. Thus, if a letter requires action, it is decided at the time the letter is read.

3. **Reports of Special Committees.** This brings up matters

43

which have been referred to a special committee for investigation and report.

4. **Special Orders.** Here is brought up any subject which has been postponed to this meeting and **made a special order.** This means that it has been given the **right of way** over all other business except the reports. To make a special order of a subject requires a two-thirds vote, since it suspends the ordinary order of business previously adopted.

Another way to make a special order is to adopt a program for a meeting, which assigns a certain subject to a certain hour.

5. **Unfinished Business.** At this point is brought up any questions left undecided by adjournment of the previous meeting, provided the regular meetings of the organization are as often as quarterly. Unfinished business also includes subjects postponed to this meeting but not made a special order.

6. **New Business.** This is the place to introduce any other business which may properly come before the assembly.

Every meeting may not include all these steps. A special meeting, unless the by-laws permit otherwise, should consider only the purposes for which it was called. However, unless the by-laws specifically prohibit, after the business stated in the call has been disposed of, other urging business requiring immediate attention may be presented.

In advance of a meeting the secretary should prepare for the presiding officer an Order of Business, filling in the specific subjects to be brought up at that meeting. For example, under Item No. 2 would be listed the letters to be read and the committees which are to report, and under the other items the exact nature of the business to be presented. This outline is the Orders of the Day.

If the meeting gets "off the road," it is the right of any member to call attention to it and ask that the regular order be followed. This is the call for the Orders of the Day.

There are two times when a call for the Orders of the Day would be in order: (1) When the time has come for a **special order** to be taken up and the chair either overlooks it or allows the discussion of other business to continue; (2) if some item of business is introduced at a time when business of that nature is not in order (for example, if a motion that is properly new business is introduced before a question which should come up under unfinished business).

So important is it that a meeting shall follow the established order, that the call for the Orders of the Day is one of the few motions which can be made at times even when another has the floor. Also, it requires no second and no recognition by the chair.

It must be realized that the call for the Orders of the Day, while it has this high privilege of interruption, does not itself oblige the meeting to drop the business before it. However, the chairman must either state the proper business or take a vote to decide immediately whether the meeting will take up the regular order or not. It requires a **negative** vote of two-thirds to refuse to take up the regular order. Thus, an affirmative vote of more than one-third can compel a meeting to cease discussion of a subject which interferes with the regular order of business and take up the business which is proper at that time.

If the call for the Orders of the Day seems a motion infrequently made, it is not because the average assembly seldom departs from the proper routine, but more probably because such departures are usually permitted by general consent. A single objection requires a vote to determine whether the deviation shall be permitted, unless the proper business is immediately taken up.

Order of Business Should Be Followed

CHAPTER XIII

SOME INCIDENTAL AND MISCELLANEOUS MOTIONS

Preceding chapters have dealt with three classes of motions: (1) the main motion (Chapter V), which includes all the motions which bring a proposition before the assembly; (2) subsidiary motions (Chapter VI), which are the "tools" with which the assembly disposes of the main motion; and (3) privileged motions (Chapter XI), which have nothing to do with either main or subsidiary motions but which have the privilege of interrupting discussion of business in order to allow the assembly to attend to some matter relating to the meeting itself.

There is a fourth class of motions called Incidental Motions, because they are **incidental** to, that is, they arise out of, the consideration of some question. They are not so readily "simplified" as the other classes of motions because, while they are all "incidental" to business, they differ in their uses, the motions to which they may be applied and which may be applied to them, and they have no rank among themselves. They are alike in one respect: because they interrupt discussion or decision of the question to which they are incidental and must be decided before it, they are undebatable (Fundamental No. 7). The only exception is an appeal in certain cases.

To use the factory illustration again (See Chapters VI and XI), it is as if a workman while engaged upon some job were given instructions by the foreman regarding the work or his use of the tools.

The following table lists the most common incidental motions together with the chief rules regarding them:

	Must be seconded	Can be amended	Other subsidiary motions	Vote
Point of order	No	No	No	Decided by chair
Appeal	Yes	No	Yes	Majority (a tie vote sustains the chair)
Objection to consideration	No	No	No	Two-thirds (negative to sustain objection)
Division of question ...	°Yes	Yes	Yes	°Majority
Division of assembly ..	No	No	No	None
Division of assembly (and count)	Yes	No	No	Majority
Motions relating to voting	Yes	Yes	Yes	Majority
Motions relating to nominations	Yes	Yes	Yes	°°Majority
Withdraw a motion ...	No	No	No	Majority (unless granted by common consent)
Suspend the rules	Yes	No	No	Two-thirds (except standing rules, which may be suspended by majority)

°If resolutions relate to different subjects, they must be divided on request of a single member. If they relate to the same subject and yet each part can stand alone, to separate them takes a regular motion and vote.

°°The motion to close nominations takes a two-thirds vote (Fundamental No. 11).

A **point of order** is made or **question of order** is raised by a member who thinks there is a breach of rules. It is usually decided by the chair, and from this decision any two members may **appeal,** one making the appeal and the other seconding it.

The **objection to consideration** of a question is in order only at the time a question is first introduced, before it is debated. Once debate has started, obviously to object to its consideration would be absurd. The objection can be made by one member, but to sustain it requires a negative vote of two-thirds on the query as stated by the chair, "Shall the question be considered?"

The **division of the question** is a demand or a motion that a resolution be divided into two or more parts for separate consideration. The **division of the assembly** is a means whereby the affirmative and negative votes on a question are divided from each other. It is (1) a demand (needing no second) that a rising vote be taken, or (2) a motion (needing a second) that a rising vote be taken and **counted**.

Motions relating to voting merely specify the way the vote is to be taken (See Chapter XV); and **motions relating to nominations** are used to close and reopen nominations.

To **suspend the rules** may be necessary on occasion. When made it should specify the purpose for which rules are to be suspended and it requires a two-thirds vote, except that Standing Rules, because they are adopted at any meeting, may be suspended at any meeting by a majority vote. Rules in the by-laws naturally cannot be suspended even by unanimous vote, but must be amended or rescinded according to the provisions in the by-laws—usually two-thirds vote with notice.

If the foregoing list of motions and the rules applicable to them seem without "rhyme or reason" there is no need to spend time memorizing them. When any of the motions arise, just apply the rule of common sense. For example, is it not obvious that **one person** should be able to raise a point of order? Hence it needs no second to require the attention of the chair. An **appeal** from the decision of the chair, however, should logically be only upon demand of **two** members. The motion granting permission to withdraw a motion that has been made, seconded, and stated, requires no second, since the one who makes the motion granting permission to withdraw is really seconding the one who requested permission.

Also, with regard to amendability. The division of a question, and motions as to the method of voting and making nominations, include points about which the assembly may have differing opinions and it should have the right to make suitable changes before adopting such motions.

These incidental motions have no rank among themselves. They all take precedence over the main motion, of course. Some of them take precedence over subsidiary motions except, usually, the motion to lay on the table. All yield to privileged motions, unless the question out of which they arise is a privileged motion, in which case they take precedence over it. To illustrate: Even though the motion to adjourn (privileged) has

been made and stated and even put, a motion relating to the way the vote is to be taken is in order and would have to be decided before taking the vote on the motion to adjourn.

Four other miscellaneous motions frequently used are:

Ratify	Incidental Main Motion
Rescind	Incidental Main Motion
Take from the Table	Unclassified
Reconsider	Unclassified

To **take from the table** brings before the assembly a question laid on the table at the same or at a previous meeting. Like the motion to lay on the table, it is undebatable and unamendable. When a motion is taken from the table it comes back in exactly the same condition in which it was laid on the table.

Because the motion to lay on the table has the high privilege (see Chapter VII) of laying aside a question by a simple majority without debate, presumably for more urgent business, the motion to take from the table has the right of way over any other main motions that have not actually been stated by the chair, provided it is made when business of that class is in order. In organizations meeting as often as quarterly the effect of the motion to lay on the table lasts only until the end of the next session. In others it ends with the same session at which it was ordered. Consequently, the motion to take from the table must be made within those limits. Practically, this is no hindrance to the transaction of business, since after it is too late to take from the table, the motion which was tabled may be introduced again as "new business."

The motion **to ratify** is used when it is necessary to confirm action taken by a board or committee or by an officer in excess of authority, or when urgent business has been transacted at a meeting without a quorum present. In both cases, a motion to ratify adopted at a later meeting of the assembly will legalize the action. It is the same as a motion to approve or confirm.

The motions to reconsider and rescind are treated separately in the following chapter.

CHAPTER XIV

A SECOND OPPORTUNITY—
RECONSIDER AND RESCIND

It is never too late to mend. Even an organization may make mistakes; and, if it does, it should have the means for correcting them. Changes desired in the by-laws can be made only by following the rules provided in the by-laws for such changes. In other business, however, revision is usually accomplished by one of the two motions "to reconsider" and "to rescind."

Similar as these may seem in their purpose, in their details they are quite unlike. Perhaps no motions are more frequently misused or misunderstood. It is the mark of a good parliamentarian to know when to use one and when the other and how the vote should be taken on each. However, by getting a basic understanding of their purposes, it is possible for any member to gain a clear picture of these motions.

Difference in Effect. First note the difference in the **wording** of the motions. One is to **reconsider** the **vote**; the other is to **rescind** the **motion** or **action**. This shows plainly that the motions apply to different things. To reconsider, if carried, **reopens** the **vote** on some question previously decided. To rescind **wipes out** altogether the previous motion to which it applies.

In an earlier chapter a motion was likened to the contents of a box. The vote on the motion closed the cover. The motion to reconsider, if carried, merely reopens the cover and brings the contents before the assembly in the same condition as before. The motion to rescind, if carried, throws the entire box away, including contents.

When they can be made. The motion to reconsider can be made only on the day that the vote in question was taken or on the next day, a recess or a holiday not counting as a day. This means that in the average organization it can be made only the same day, since few deliberative organizations meet two days in succession. In a convention or gathering which meets for several days, the "next day" rule of course applies.

The motion to reconsider may be made at any time during the meeting at which the vote was taken or on the next day even when another motion is pending, or after the vote to adjourn has been made and carried, provided the meeting is not actually declared adjourned. The **making** of the motion thus has great privilege, due to its purpose to protect the majority against an unrepresentative decision. The motion is not **voted on**, however, until "called up," which may be later in the session or, in organizations meeting regularly as often as quarterly, at the next session. If the motion to reconsider is made at a time when it would interrupt business, it is not "called up" for vote until after the immediate business is decided.

Be Sure to Choose the Right One for the Purpose

The motion to reconsider cannot be applied to votes on motions that can be renewed after progress in debate, such as the motion to adjourn, nor when other motions would accomplish the same purpose. For example, it cannot be applied to the motion to lay on the table. In this case, the motion to take from the table would accomplish the same purpose.

The motion to rescind may be made at any time: on the day the action in question was ordered or any day thereafter, provided that nothing has been done that cannot be undone. It cannot be made if the same purpose can be accomplished by "calling up" a motion to reconsider which has previously been made. Neither the motion to reconsider nor rescind can be made if action has been taken as a result of the previous vote which is in the nature of a contract and the other party has been notified.

Who can make them. The motion to reconsider must be made by one who voted on the prevailing side in the vote to be reconsidered. This is to indicate that there has been some change of opinion. A rule of parliamentary law is that no question, after once being decided, can come up at the same meeting in the same form under the same circumstances (Fundamental No. 9). The motion to reconsider brings up the **same question** as was decided, and in the **same form,** but the **circumstances** are **different** in that one who formerly voted for the motion now apparently wishes to change his vote. In compliance with this fundamental, however, once the motion to reconsider itself has been decided it cannot be renewed in connection with the same motion.

The motion to rescind may be made by anyone, regardless of how he voted on the question to be rescinded. This does not violate the fundamental "No second time in the same form," because the form of the motion is directly opposite to the form of the previous motion.

Are they debatable? The motion to reconsider is debatable when the motion to be reconsidered is debatable. It also opens the whole question to debate, because the question of reconsideration hinges upon the question to be reconsidered. Furthermore, those who may have exhausted their right to speak on the original motion are privileged to speak on the motion to reconsider. If the motion to reconsider is carried, it brings the former motion back **in the same condition,** and those who, when it was previously discussed, exhausted for that day their right to debate the motion have no right to discuss it further. The opportunity for such members to debate is during discussion of the motion to reconsider.

The motion to rescind, being a main motion, is fully debatable unless the debate is limited or closed by one of the motions for that purpose.

What vote decides. A majority vote decides the motion to reconsider. Since it is made the same day, or the next day, it is assumed that all interested in defending their side of the vote in question are present and ready to defend. It is also assumed that there has been a change of sentiment, otherwise one who voted on the prevailing side would not make the motion.

The motion to rescind takes a two-thirds vote unless notice of the intention to move it was made at the previous meeting or included in the call for this meeting (Fundamental No. 11). This notice serves as a warning to absent members who may be interested. Without notice, the two-thirds vote to a certain extent protects the interests of absentees by insuring that more than a majority are ready to repeal the motion.

Result of adoption. If the motion to reconsider is carried, it brings before the assembly again a motion previously voted on in the same form as before the vote was taken. For example, suppose a motion is made to give a lecture. A subsidiary motion is then offered to refer this question to a committee, and before this is voted on a motion is carried to postpone the question to the next meeting. Then a vote to reconsider the vote on postponement is carried. The question now recurs to the postponement to the next meeting. If this is again carried the question is settled. If lost this time, the question is on referring it to a committee. All motions which would be in order before the original vote was taken are again in order.

A motion to rescind, on the other hand, ends the matter. No further vote is taken unless a new motion on the same subject in changed form is presented. The former motion cannot be erased from the minutes, but all other effects are eliminated.

The motion to reconsider is sometimes made with the provision that it be entered on the minutes to be "called up" at the next meeting. This is permissible and is the form to use when a motion has been adopted at an unrepresentative meeting ordering action which some members may not feel would be approved by a majority of the members. The motion to reconsider made and seconded and "entered on the minutes" **prevents any action** on the motion to be reconsidered until the motion to reconsider the vote is **called up** and **decided.** The motion to reconsider in this form can be applied only to votes which finally dispose of a main motion, since its purpose is to delay action; and only final votes on a main motion commit the assembly to a position regarding proposed action. Also, it can be made only on the day the vote to be reconsidered is taken, and it cannot be called up on that day.

If one who conscientiously voted against a certain action believes that the action is not representative of the sentiment of the membership **he may change his vote** before the result is announced in order to move to reconsider and enter on the minutes.

Illustrations: Suppose a motion has been carried to rent a hall for a year. It may be reconsidered at that meeting or on the next day, provided one who voted for the motion moves to reconsider. It may be rescinded, but this motion would take two-thirds vote, there being no previous notice given. If notice is given, the action may be rescinded by a majority vote at the next meeting, but in the meantime the lease might be signed. If a member thinks the action would not be supported by the majority at a representative meeting, by voting for it he can move reconsideration and have it entered on the minutes to be "called up" at the next meeting. The lease cannot then be signed until after the next meeting, and then only if the motion to reconsider, being called up, results in confirmation of the former action. Or, if the lease is not actually signed before the next meeting, at that time the action may be rescinded by two-thirds vote without notice, but it is too late to reconsider. If the lease has been signed, it is too late to rescind.

CHAPTER XV

"ALL THOSE IN FAVOR . . ."

The vote is the most important step in a deliberative assembly. It is the means whereby the group, no matter how large or small, determines its composite opinion on the question before it.

Voting is also the most valuable right of a member. He may not be able to sway his fellow members by his eloquence, or convince them by reason, but when it comes time to make the decision, his vote is of equal value with any other (Fundamental No. 2).

Naturally, so important a prerogative is safeguarded by parliamentary law. An organization may invite outsiders to its meetings and permit them to take part in discussion, may even select a non-member to preside, unless its by-laws prohibit. But **only members can vote.** The right to vote cannot be taken from a member except by expulsion or suspension, unless the by-laws permit it for some specific cause. Nor can a member be compelled to vote. He has the right to change his vote up to the time the result is announced, because no question is finally settled until the result of the vote is announced.

There are five ways the vote may be taken: (1) viva voce (pronounced **vi-va vo-se**) or by show of hands, (2) rising, (3) general consent, (4) ballot, (5) roll call.

Viva voce means "by voice" and is the method generally used in an ordinary meeting. It is sometimes called the "ayes and noes" because the vote is taken first by those in favor of a motion responding "aye" to the question of the chair, followed by those opposed saying "no." In some organizations, instead of using the "ayes" and "noes" it is the custom for the chair to ask those in favor to "raise the right hand," and then for those opposed to do likewise. Robert classifies the show of hands as a form of viva voce voting, although it may be used in small assemblies when a counted vote is necessary.

From the difference in volume between the "ayes" and "noes," or the difference in the number of hands raised, the chair decides which side "has it" and declares the motion carried or lost.

Rising Vote. Sometimes the chair is "in doubt" regarding the result. He may then request those in favor to rise and, after they are seated, ask those opposed to rise. If there remains any doubt the chair may order a count.

Even though the chair may not be in doubt after a viva voce and declares the motion carried or lost, if **any member** doubts the result he may compel a rising vote by calling out from his seat, "Division."

Some presiding officers make it a practice to count every rising vote. In an assembly which does not have more than a hundred present this is a good practice, but it is not a compulsory. If the chair does not have the votes counted, a majority may order a count. In some meetings it is the custom for the chair and the secretary to count the votes, acting by common consent as self-appointed tellers. Generally, however, and particularly in a large group, it is better to appoint tellers and thus avoid all possibility of criticism of unfairness. A rising vote on a question requiring a two-thirds vote should be counted, unless it is apparent to everyone that those who rise first are many more than the required number. A counted vote should be recorded in the minutes.

General consent. This is a method frequently used to decide matters concerning which there is not likely to be much difference of opinion. Many members observe business transacted in this way without being aware that it is actually a form of voting. For example, the chair says, "If there is no objection, the minutes will stand approved as read," or "If there is no objection, the change in the motion will be made," or "If there is no objection, the windows will be opened." If silence greets his statement it is the same as if by a unanimous vote the meeting had adopted a motion to approve the minutes or amend the motion or open the windows. The chair then says, "The minutes are approved," or "The motion as amended is approved," or state whatever is ordered by general consent.

Business may often be speeded up by this method. Rules are of little use when everyone is of one mind and there is no minority to be protected. A meeting may even be adjourned without a vote, provided there is no objection. Anything that can be done by a majority vote or a two-thirds vote without notice can be done by unanimous consent, except such votes as are required by rules to be taken by ballot. The point that members should realize is that unanimity is the essence of this vote. A single objection obliges the chair to put the question by viva voce or whatever other method of voting may be ordered. If, when unanimous consent is asked for some action, a member feels that it is not a wise thing to do, he should voice his objection. There may be others who feel the same way and the objection obliges a motion to be presented which offers opportunity for the expression of opinions on both sides.

Ballot. The vote by ballot is used wherever secrecy is essential. The by-laws should stipulate its use in the election of officers, or the discipline of members. On any question where secrecy would help in bringing out the true opinions of those voting, a ballot vote is helpful and a majority can order it taken. In ballot voting, blanks do not count as votes. A majority vote by ballot is a majority of votes cast—just as in other methods of voting—unless the by-laws stipulate otherwise. The members present are usually counted and compared with the number of votes cast. But this is to be sure that there are no more votes than members present.

Roll Call (or yeas and nays). This method of voting is usually confined to legislative bodies. It requires the members present to answer "yes" or "no" as their names are called, and the vote to be recorded. It is of little use in an ordinary deliberative body unless, perhaps, it is desired to put the members of a board, for example, on record so there can be no dispute later as to how they voted on a question. To be of value, the rules should permit this vote if used to be called for by a relatively small number, such as one-fifth, since the majority in favor of an action would probably see no reason for recording the vote.

The How and Why of the Two-Thirds Vote. The majority decides ordinary questions (Fundamental No. 10). But there may arise certain questions which, in fairness to absentees or to a minority or to individual members, should take more than a mere majority.

To protect the interest of those who may have been present when a certain motion was adopted and who feel strongly in favor of it, it requires a two-thirds vote (unless previous notice is given) to rescind or change any such motion. To rescind or amend by-laws requires the two-thirds vote **and** notice.

In order to protect the right of members to introduce business, debate, vote, and have the meeting conducted according to rules, it takes a two-thirds vote to prevent consideration of a question, to close or limit debate, to close nominations, or polls, to do anything contrary to the established rules of order. To expel from office or membership requires a two-thirds vote **with notice.**

It takes an alert chairman and an alert membership to be sure that all votes calling for two-thirds are thus handled. Assume that a motion has been in force for some time, establishing certain procedure. Innocently enough, a motion is presented, not referring to the previous motion, yet conflicting with it. It is the same as a motion to amend or rescind the previous motion and, unless notice was given at the previous meeting, it calls for a two-thirds vote. If, however, attention is not called to the error at the time, the matter stands as decided. Note, however, that to **amend** a motion requiring a two-thirds vote requires only a majority vote. The only amendment which requires a two-thirds vote is the motion to amend by-laws, which is really a main motion. On motions requiring a two-thirds vote a rising vote should always be taken.

Silence Gives Consent. Precious as is the privilege of voting, it must be exercised to be of use. Paradoxically enough, under certain conditions, the failure to vote actually "counts" in the result, although it is not actually counted. Unless the by-laws require a vote to be a majority "of those present" or any other proportion "of those present," a person who fails to vote is not counted. Yet the actual effect is as if a vote had been cast for the prevailing side.

Suppose, for example, in a meeting of a hundred persons a rising vote is taken on a question. Fifteen vote in favor. Twenty vote against. Twenty being a majority of those voting, the motion is lost even though the total is less than half those present. It is as if the other 65 persons voted against the motion, even though the honest opinion of many of them lay in the other direction. Or, in a board of 10 members (all being present) a question is put requiring a unanimous decision. Three persons are silent. The rest vote "aye." The vote is as unanimous as if all voted "aye." Do not refrain from voting, thinking it doesn't count. It most certainly does "count."

Their Most Prized Privilege

CHAPTER XVI

USES AND DUTIES OF COMMITTEES

"Good Morning! . . . Have you heard the report which the chairman of our committee intends to make? . . . . You haven't? . . . I wonder why he doesn't call a committee meeting. . . . I think I shall telephone the other members and find out what they think. . . . Perhaps we can decide upon something and have a report ready to submit at the club meeting in case we do not agree with that of the chairman."

An imaginary telephone conversation, of course, yet plausible. It illustrates several breaches of sound committee procedure. A chairman should not take it upon himself to do the work of other members of a committee. If the assembly wishes the thought of **one** person it would appoint a committee of **one**. A chairman **may not present** a report unless it is approved in a committee meeting by at least a majority of a committee. A committee cannot agree to anything except in a regular meeting unless **all** agree. If a committee chairman does not or will not call a meeting, any **two** members of the committee may do so.

Members of committees and boards will do well to read frequently the relevant pages of Robert's Rules of Order, Revised, which set forth the proper procedure of committees. Answers to some of the questions frequently raised are as follows:

Who appoints the committee and chairman? (1) The by-laws or the motion to commit may give this power to the chair; (2) if there is no rule in the by-laws, the assembly may elect the members of a committee or direct how it shall be done; (3) whoever appoints the committee has the power to name the chairman of the committee and also to fill any vacancies that may occur. If the chair appoints, the first-named member is chairman. In any other case, if a specific person is not named, the first named acts as temporary chairman until the committee elects someone or, by taking no action, consents to the temporary chairman acting as the permanent.

When is a committee appointed? Immediately after the motion to commit is adopted, only privileged questions having the right to intervene. If the chair appoints and wishes time to make selections, he should so state, but the appointments should be announced before the meeting adjourns. The chair cannot appoint after a meeting adjourns unless specifically authorized to do so.

What should govern the appointment? A committee should preferably be an odd number of members, thereby simplifying the problem of securing a majority vote. A committee selected to recommend on a controversial subject should include both friends and foes of the proposition. If selected to carry out an order already adopted, the committee should be composed of supporters of the undertaking.

Who notifies the committee? The secretary notifies the committee chairman in writing, giving the date of the action, the exact wording of the motion which referred it, and, if it is a special committee, the names of the members of the committee and when it is to report.

Who organizes the committee? After its election or appointment a committee is called together by its chairman. If no chairman has been chosen the first named member acts as chairman until the committee elects one. If the chairman neglects to call a meeting when necessary, any two members may do so.

What may a committee do? It may discuss the question referred to it in an informal way. If a motion is made in committee the maker need not rise and it needs no second. Debate is unlimited. Every member may speak as often as he can secure recognition. A committee may change its mind as often as it wishes. That is, it can reconsider a vote it has previously taken, at any time before submitting its report. To reconsider requires only a majority, if all who previously voted on the prevailing side are present. If not, it takes a two-thirds vote. A committee may make any recommendations to the organization about the subject referred to it, provided they are agreed to by a majority of the committee. It may keep a record of its meetings for its own information, but these are destroyed when the question under consideration is disposed of.

Note. The motion which refers a subject to a committee may include the provision "with power to act," in which case the committee may take any action it sees fit and the assembly is bound by the action.

What may not a committee do? A committee must not change its instructions or depart from them. If a committee wishes to do anything exceeding its instructions or contrary to them it must report back to the assembly and secure permission. It may not do anything to the question referred to it unless given power to do so. Its activities are restricted to investigating facts and **recommending** such changes or action as it considers advisable.

Committee Must Not Depart From Instructions

What must a committee do? It must follow instructions of the assembly. If a special committee or newly elected standing committee, it must meet as soon as practicable after it is appointed in order to organize. At every meeting it must have a quorum, which is a majority of its members, unless the organization fixes a specific number. It must report to the assembly at the time specified; and, if it recommends action, should submit resolutions to carry out its recommendations.

How does a committee report? It may report orally on resolutions referred to it. As a general rule, however, reports are in writing. The report must be agreed to by a majority; if in writing, all who agree should sign, unless the chairman is empowered to sign for the committee. The chairman presents the report, reading it, if written, and then handing it to the presiding officer or to the secretary.

If the report is for information only, no action is needed. If the report makes a recommendation, the chairman of the committee should move that it be adopted. If a minority of the committee wishes to present its views it may do so, if there is no objection by any member of the assembly. If objection is made permission must be granted by vote. There is no action taken on this minority report **unless** a motion is made to substitute it for the majority report.

Note: Helpful information regarding the functions of committees and the rules regarding the motion to commit or refer may be found in Chapter IX entitled, "Delegating Duties."

CHAPTER XVII

COMMITTEE OF WHOLE, AND BOARDS

The preceding chapter pointed out that among the advantages of committee consideration are the unrestricted debate and the fact that no permanent record of proceedings is kept. On occasion, such as considering by-laws before adopting them, or some matter of a nature which is likely to require considerable discussion, the entire assembly, in order to gain these conveniences and, in some cases, to eliminate outsiders, may act as a "committee of the whole." The motion to do this is "that the assembly convene as a committee of the whole to consider," specifying the subject to be thus treated.

As soon as this motion is adopted the meeting becomes a committee. The motion "to go into a committee of the whole" might include designating those who are to serve as chairman and clerk of the committee or indicate how they are to be appointed. For instance, the motion might be, "I move the assembly convene as a committee of the whole to consider . . . and that the chairman of the assembly appoint the chairman and clerk of the committee," or "that Mr. ——— serve as chairman of the committee and Mr. ——— as clerk."

The presiding officer of the assembly may serve as chairman of the committee if the assembly desires, but it is usually better to select someone else. The presiding officer of the assembly has no more right to assume the chair in the committee than to appoint himself chairman of any other committee. Members may speak as often as they can secure recognition but must rise and obtain the floor the same as in the regular meeting. As a matter of courtesy, however, a member should not speak a second time, if another who has not yet spoken desires the floor. The committee cannot close debate or lay the question on the table, or refer it to any other committee. Like any other committee it can consider only the question committed to it and recommend action with or without changes.

When the committee has completed its consideration it does not adjourn, but "rises and reports." The assembly then reconvenes as before. The regular presiding officer resumes the chair and the chairman of the committee of the whole reports to the assembly the action recommended by the committee of the whole and moves its adoption. If the question committed is a resolution and amendments have been made by the committee of the whole, the assembly may adopt the amendments as a whole, unless a separate vote is asked on one or more of them. There should be no need for debate since the members of the assembly and the committee of the whole are identical, but debate and further change are of course permissible.

**The Meeting Becomes
a Committee**

The quorum of a committee of the whole is the same as that of the assembly. If a committee finds itself short of a quorum, it has no right to consider the business further, but should rise and report that fact. The assembly then adjourns.

There are two other ways in which small organizations may secure some of the advantages of the committee of the whole without the routine of actually convening as a committee. One is to move "to sit **as if in** committee of the whole." This permits free discussion with the regular chairman in the chair. The freedom of discussion ceases as soon as any motion is made other than to amend the motion being considered. The chair then announces the changes in the question that have been voted while sitting as if in committee of the whole, and the meeting proceeds to adopt the amendments in regular form. The secretary takes notes of proceedings while acting as if in committee of the whole, but they should not be entered in the minutes.

A still simpler method is called "informal consideration." This is accomplished by the motion that "the question be considered informally." If carried, the debate on the main motion and its amendments becomes unlimited as if in committee. As soon as a motion is made that disposes of the main motion temporarily or permanently, the informal consideration automatically ceases. No report is necessary by the chair. A record is kept of all proceedings during informal consideration, the only "informality" being in the debate.

The question may arise, Which of the three forms of consideration is best? That depends principally upon the size of the assembly and, to a less extent, the nature of the question. A very large group should go into the committee of the whole if it wishes to consider a question freely and without record. In smaller groups also this may be best in dealing with a question of a delicate nature, but as a rule the other two forms are better, informal consideration being simpler and therefore best suited to very small societies.

The Board of Directors or Trustees. As mentioned before, a board is a form of committee. It has, however, certain characteristics which differentiate it sharply from ordinary committees.

A board should be established by the by-laws. Its members are officers of the organization. The by-laws designate their number, their term of office, and the method of election. The by-laws may establish rules for the board or the rules may be left for the board to determine.

The powers of boards vary greatly among organizations. A body which meets only once a year may find it expedient to give great powers to the board which acts for it through the year. An organization whose members reside in one community and which can meet quarterly or monthly, may well reserve to itself more rights, since it may attend to much of its business at its meetings.

The board is bound by the rules of the organization, and can do nothing contrary to them. Unless the by-laws state otherwise, the organization may at any time review the actions of the board, and, if it chooses, reverse them. On the other hand, once having given the board certain powers, the organization cannot take them away nor exercise any authority contrary to them, except by rescinding or amending the by-laws or rules which granted the power.

The proceedings in a board may be as formal as in a regular assembly or as informal as in a committee, depending upon the size of the board, its rules and the attitude of its members. In a board of a dozen members or less, the meetings may be conducted like committee meetings. For example, motions need not be seconded; members may speak as often as they choose (or as frequently as "good form" and the rights of others are not interfered with); and the chairman, if he wishes, may enter into the discussion and vote. However, a board is not restricted to the motions used in a committee. It has all the range of motions the parent body has. Action may be taken only at a regular meeting or a properly called special meeting.

A majority is a quorum unless the rules state otherwise. Even if all the members agree to action outside a meeting, it must be ratified at a proper meeting. A permanent record must be kept of all action taken by a board.

A board may appoint subcommittees of its own members and

other committees, as empowered by the parent organization. A board of a large national organization, whose members live at widely separated points, may (if authorized by the by-laws) select an executive committee of members of the board. The executive committee, or any other subcommittee appointed by the board, is responsible to the board, not to the organization. The board is responsible to the parent body not only for its own acts but for those by any subcommittee appointed by the board.

CHAPTER XVIII

PRACTICE MAKES PERFECT

The best way to learn is to do. This is as true in acquiring parliamentary proficiency as in gaining skill in art, music, athletics, or any other line of endeavor. A dissertation on swimming, however chockfull of good ideas it may be, will never alone make a good swimmer of the one who reads it. One who wishes to become an expert parliamentarian will own a parliamentary manual and refer to it frequently. He will do well to make it a habit to look up a point which has been questioned, or upon which he is not sure, as soon as possible, just as he would consult a dictionary when in the least doubt about spelling a word. It would be advantageous also to own a good parliamentary text-book or course of study with its valuable drill material and answers to questions. Merely reading these, however, will not make him an efficient parliamentarian.

A member of an organization may, of course, learn much through observation while attending meetings. He may learn still more by taking an active part in proceedings. Nevertheless, however attentive he may be, it is not likely that these activities alone will give him that extra margin of knowledge which renders him truly capable of presiding over a meeting or making his full contribution as a member.

It would seem that the most perplexing parliamentary problems arise suddenly. Furthermore, when they do occur, they usually involve an important question. It sometimes appears as if the really vital questions are those which bring out the greatest diversity of opinion, give rise to the most animated discussion, and often lead straight into a parliamentary tangle.

Unhappy indeed is the position of the presiding officer who faces such a crisis with a smattering of parliamentary knowledge which has been picked up at random. It is unsafe to rely upon the likelihood of business running in a groove, trusting to "get by." The truly efficient chairman or member strives to be prepared to meet any situation.

"How is such parliamentary knowledge to be gained?" may be asked. "One can't make motions in a meeting just for the practice or to test the chairman's knowledge. How is one to get actual experience in making motions and handling them, especially the less frequently needed motions?"

Small organizations might arrange special meetings for parliamentary drill, just as the varsity football team goes through practice preliminary to the big game. In large organizations this may be impractical, because only in small groups do the individuals gain fullest opportunity for active participation. An ideal group would consist of 20 to 30 members. In large organizations, therefore, members who are most interested may arrange among themselves for such practice groups.

It is a help if such a group can meet with an experienced parliamentarian who is capable of leading the discussion. The prime requisite, however, is that each one be sufficiently interested to study the readings assigned, to take his turn at presiding, and take an active part in the doings.

Readings should be assigned on phases of parliamentary law. While Robert's Rules of Order, Revised, is intended as a reference book rather than a text, it has, at the end of the book, some lesson outlines which may serve as a basis for study. There are good courses available which present a greater amount of explanatory material and are better organized for class work. The group may meet as a hypothetical club to dispose of hypothetical business. Each member should come prepared to offer motions, preferably those that give opportunity for procedure not ordinarily encountered. It should be the aim to test the knowledge of the chairman by offering motions out of order and in order.

The members take turns presiding for periods of, for example, 10 minutes. At the end of each period, there is opportunity for general discussion, the members having taken notes of errors or questions. Or the discussion may be held along with the drill, anyone raising a question when an error is noticed or information is desired.

Such practice group meetings may be made something of a game, after the style of the old-fashioned spelling bee. Each presiding officer might be allowed to continue until a parliamentary error is committed, when the next in line would take his place.

It might be helpful for such a practice group to provide itself with charts, giving the essential information about motions used in parliamentary procedure. A helpful chart is one patterned after that published in Chapter XI, showing subsidiary and privileged motions. This shows the principal motions according to their rank.

Another helpful chart would be the following list of subsidiary motions and certain incidental motions:

Motions Grouped According to Purpose

To Modify Action

Amend * #
Commit (Refer to a Committee) *

To Defer Action

Postpone to a Certain Time *
Postpone and Make a Special Order (2/3) *
Lay on the Table
Commit (Refer to a Committee) *

To Bring Discussion to a Close

Previous Question (2/3)

To Limit Discussion

To Limit Debate (2/3) *

To Prevent Final Action Until the Next Meeting

Reconsider and Enter on Minutes #

To Suppress a Question

Objection to Consideration (2/3)
Postpone Indefinitely

To Consider a Second Time

Take from the Table
Reconsider #
Rescind *

Motions shaded are undebatable.

2/3 indicates that they require a 2/3 vote. Motion to rescind also requires 2/3 vote without notice.

*Indicates motions which may be amended.

Not debatable if applied to an undebatable motion. Motion to reconsider and enter on minutes is not debatable until called up.

With these two charts on the wall at every practice session, it should be easy for members to decide what motion to use to accomplish a certain purpose and for the one acting as chairman to determine whether it is in order; if it is amendable or debatable; and what vote it requires. A caution should be inserted here against depending too much on the charts. Certainly some of the sessions should be held without the charts visible, else the members will come to rely on them to such an extent that they will be at a loss without them in an actual meeting.

A closing word: Parliamentary knowledge, like any other knowledge, is best used when made to serve the best interests of the group. It becomes objectionable when flaunted at every opportunity. A meeting of an organization is for the purpose of transacting business and not for the exhibition of parliamentary knowledge, either by the presiding officer or a member.

A minor violation of procedure, if due to ignorance and if no privilege is nullified by it or if the proper business of the assembly is not interfered with, may well be overlooked. The member who rises to object at every point of departure from strict procedure is himself frequently hindering rather than helping. The discreet, unostentatious, efficient chairman will be neither officious nor lax in applying the rules of parliamentary law. The safest rule for members and officers alike is, "Fairness to all, Courtesy always,"—simply another application of that great fundamental, the Golden Rule.

INDEX

73